A Practical Guide to Watching the Universe

5th Grade Astronomy Textbook

Astronomy & Space Science

BABY PROFESSOR

EDUCATION KIDS

Have you ever tried using a telescope to view the stars or the moon in the night sky?

Well, if you haven't, using a telescope helps you to enjoy watching the shining stars and the wonderful light of the moon.

A telescope is
an essential tool
in the field of
astronomy. It makes
objects that are
far in the distance
appear closer.

In 1608, a Dutch lens maker, Hans Lippershey, invented the refractor telescope.

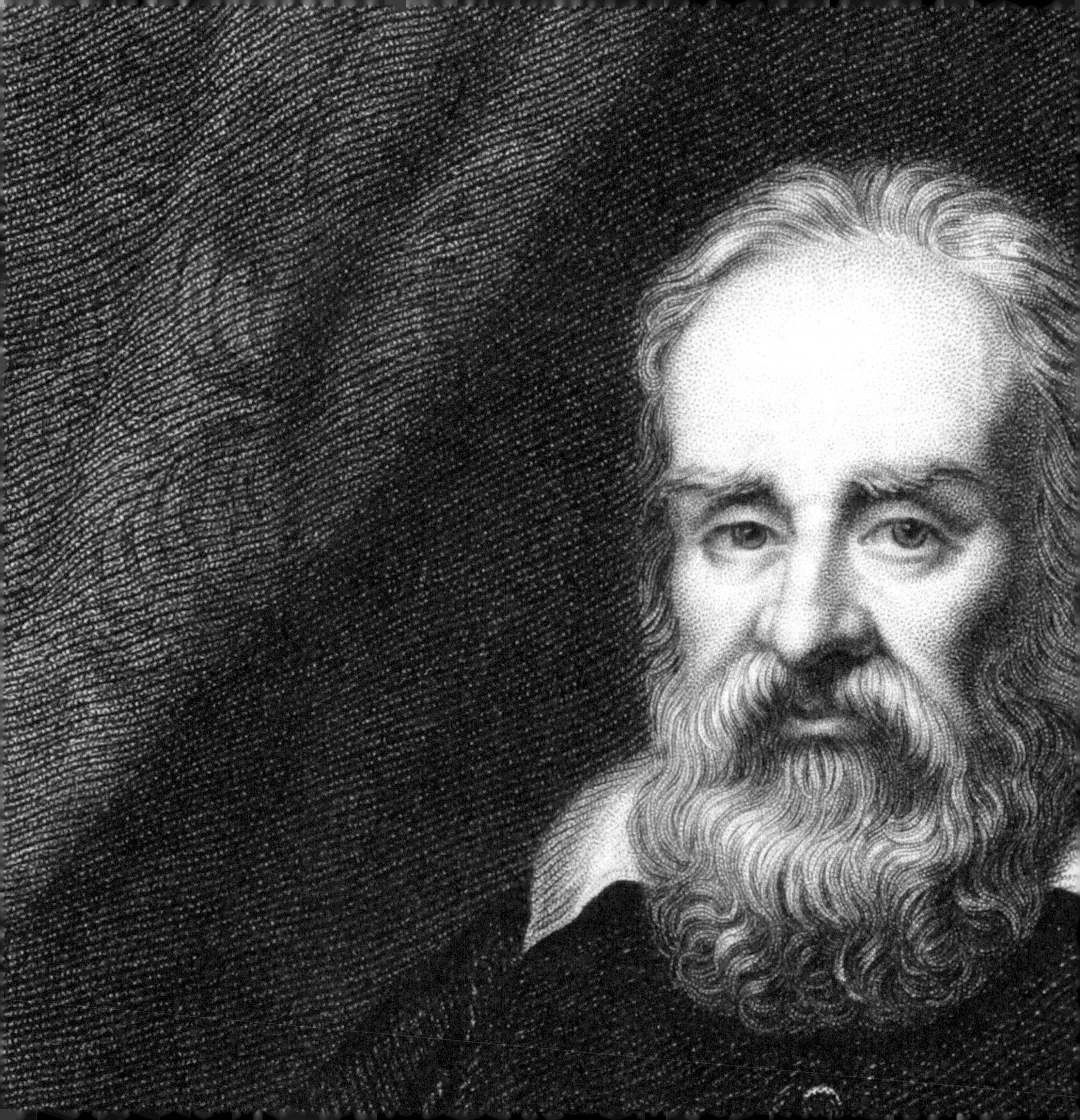

Galileo Galilei made
improvements
on the telescope
and first used it
for astronomy.

Galilei discovered
four of the moons
of Jupiter, the
Milky Way's starry
nature, and that
there are mountains
on the Moon.

In 1611, Johannes Kepler further improved the refractor telescope by using a convex lens for its eyepiece.

Isaac Newton then invented the first reflector telescope which solved the issues of working with a refractor telescope.

There are different kinds of telescope used by astronomers to study the universe. These are:

Radio Telescope - It is used by astronomers in finding stars and other objects. This can also pick up radio waves from space.

Radio telescopes can produce a photo from an object it is listening to from the noise it picks up from the specific object.

The information
received by a couple
of radio telescopes
in different places
can be merged.

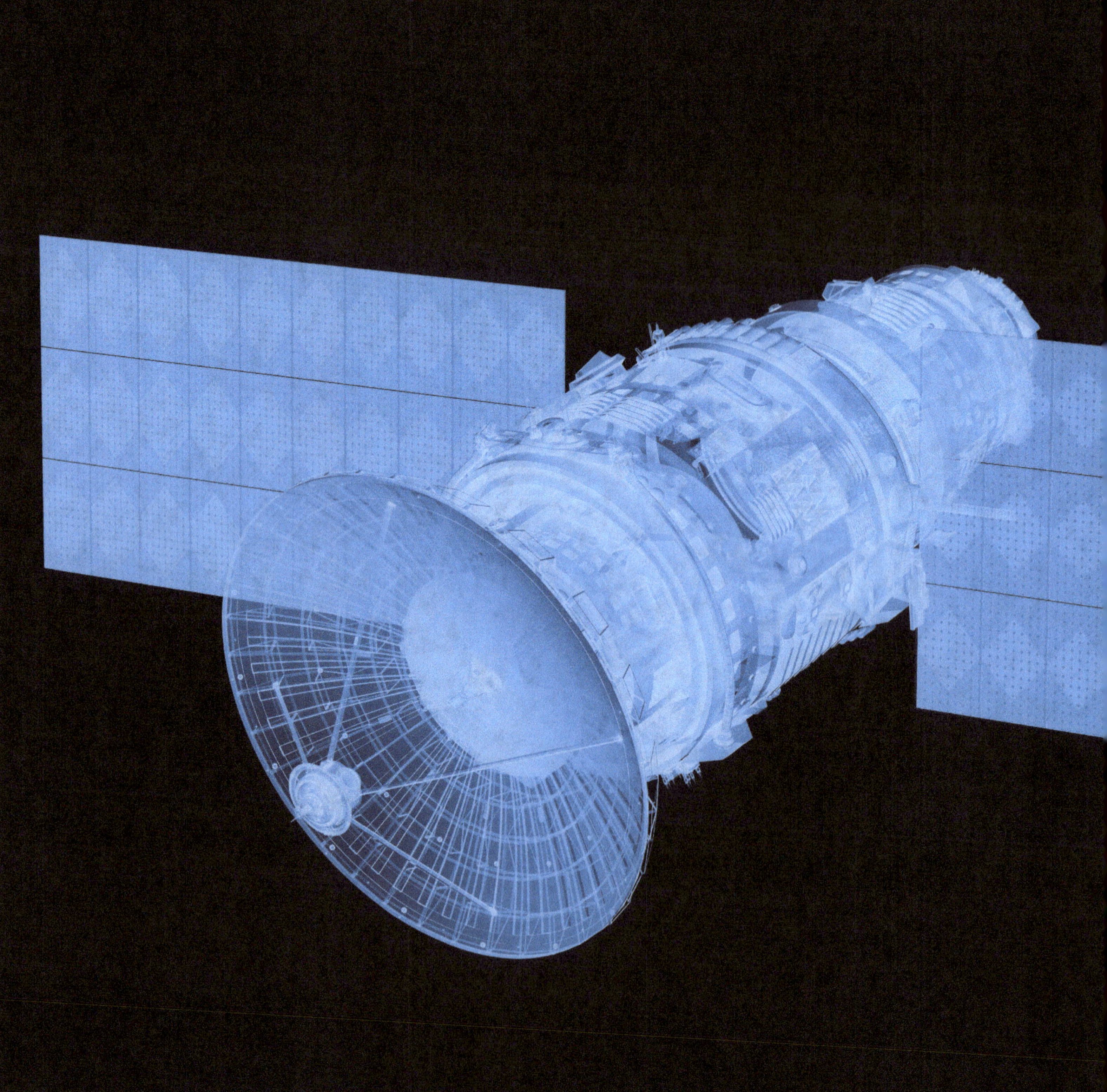

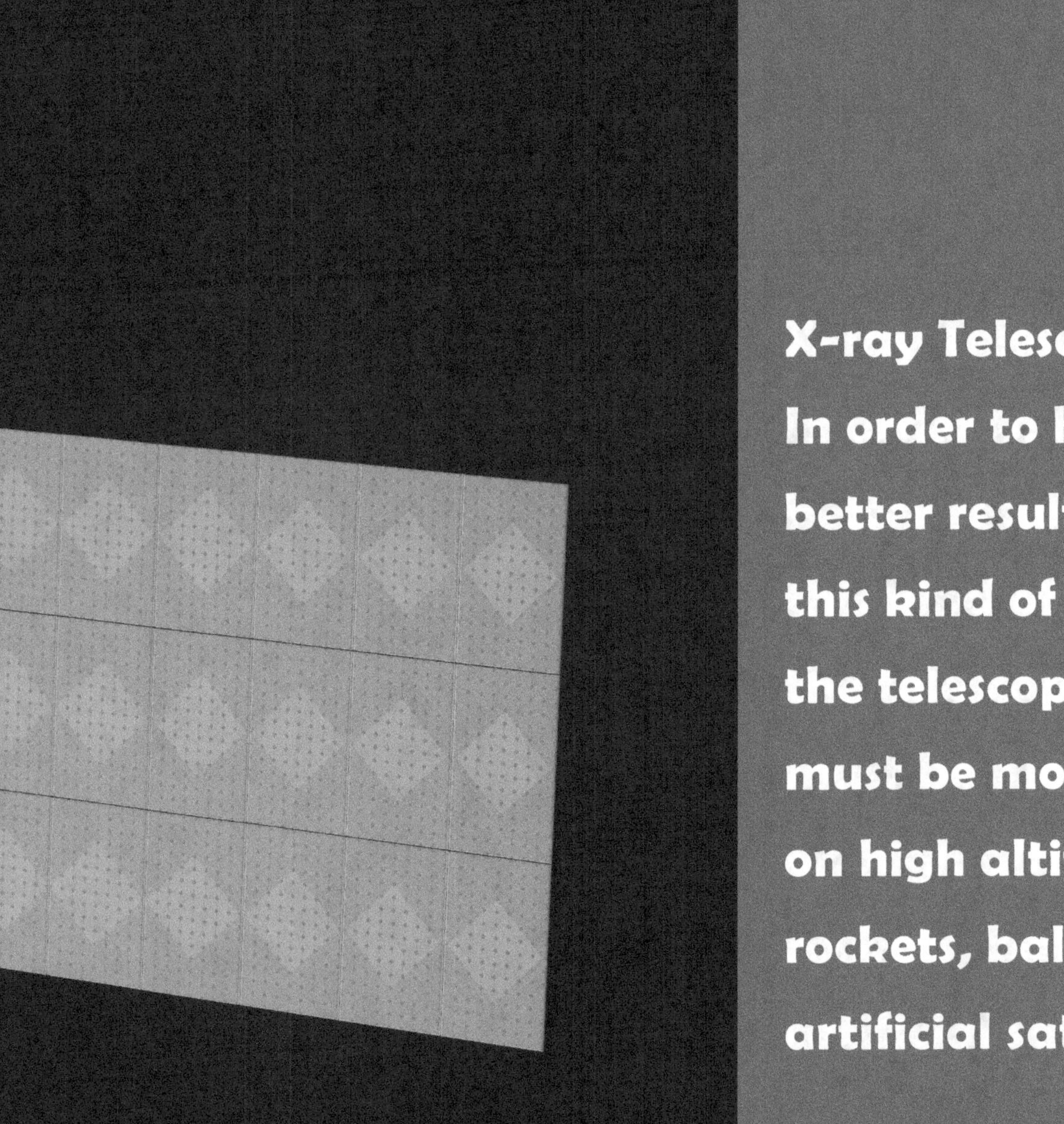

**X-ray Telescope -
In order to have a
better result in using
this kind of telescope,
the telescope
must be mounted
on high altitude
rockets, balloons or
artificial satellites.**

It works even better
when you are using
the telescope in
space. This is used
for studying the
Sun, supernovas,
and even the stars.

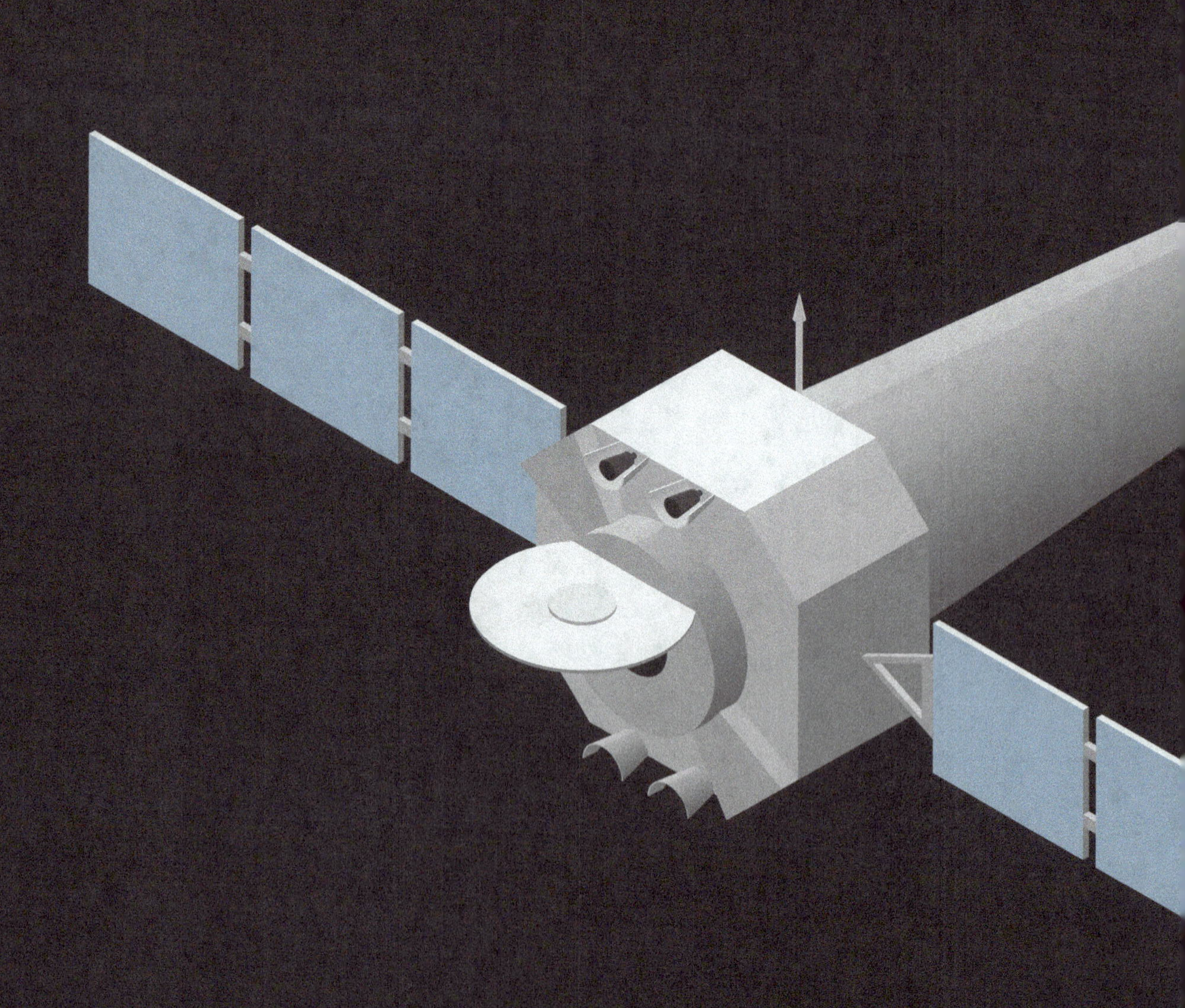

The design of this telescope is different from a conventional optical telescope.

Gamma Ray Telescope – This kind of telescope helps astronomers in confirm events such as supernovas, black holes, and pulsars.

Just like an X-ray telescope, a gamma ray telescope needs to be used in places with high altitude, or in space.

Gamma-ray telescopes are mostly carried on satellites and balloons. The first gamma-ray telescope was carried by the American satellite Explorer 11 in 1961.

**Reflector Telescope -
Isaac Newton
invented the reflector
telescope in 1668.**

This kind of telescope has mirrors in which the light bounces off so that you can see the object from a far distance. A reflector telescope is very expensive because it has to be made to a very high standard of quality.

The largest
reflecting telescope
in the world is the
Gran Telescopio
Canarias in Spain.

Refractor Telescope - Unlike a reflector telescope where it uses mirrors, a refractor telescope uses lenses to gather light.

It's like a magnifying glass but it is much better. It is used to see the moon and the planets just like a reflecting telescope but the result of a refractor is not as detailed as the reflector.

This kind of telescope isn't as expensive compared to a reflecting telescope.

Refractor telescopes should not be longer than 40 inches in order to be easy to use.

Do you know the most famous telescope in the world today?

It is the Hubble Space Telescope! It is a reflector telescope that was first launched on April 24, 1990 into space by the Space Shuttle.

It is the largest telescope invented by humans. It takes amazing images of stars and galaxies from outer space.

Today, many astronomers already use computer controlled telescopes.

Astronomers make great discoveries through the help of a telescope. Without a telescope, humanity won't be able to know what is happening in outer space.

15 X
60

Through this, we start to value the importance of astronomy, which has changed how we view the universe.

Did you enjoy reading this book? Share this to your friends.

Visit
BABY PROFESSOR
EDUCATION KIDS
www.BabyProfessorBooks.com
to download Free Baby Professor eBooks
and view our catalog of new and exciting
Children's Books